THE CORPORATE ENIGMA

WOMEN BUSINESS OWNERS
IN NEW ZEALAND

MARY K. WELSH

ACKNOWLEDGEMENTS

I would first like to thank the Fulbright Foundation for providing me with the opportunity to work, study and live within New Zealand for the past eighteen months. In addition, I would like to express my gratitude to individuals at GP Books, Consultus-NZ Ltd. and members of Zonta Auckland Club 2 for helping guarantee this book's publication. However, I would most like to thank all the individuals interviewed for this book. Without them, such a study could never have occurred.

DEDICATION

To my mother and father

ISBN: 0–477–01430–5

Designed by Lynne Ciochetto

Typeset in 11/12½ point Garamond by Saba Graphics Ltd and printed on 105 gsm matt art

CONTENTS

PREFACE:
THE CORPORATE ENIGMA

They are the business world's best-kept secret. Although thousands of women are opening and operating their own businesses in New Zealand, mystery, intrigue and an aura of "something taboo" surround their efforts. Because women business owners operate within a male-structured business world, statisticians have almost overlooked their steadily increasing numbers. Why? Economist and author Steven Solomon notes that — as in New Zealand — the United States' "entrepreneurial boom has been driven by women . . . [and] no one has really noticed it because most of the glamour is in the high tech businesses, which are usually run by men."[1] Called "invisible entrepreneurs", women business owners are encouraging their "sisters" to pierce through the mystique, and cross a new economic frontier embracing business ownership as their manifest destiny.

New Zealand's women business owners are beginning to hold a very important position in the nation's economy. At present, almost twenty-six thousand women have chosen to establish, maintain, and profit from their own start-up ventures. The United States remains the outstanding example with its three million women proprietors and predictions indicating women will constitute half of all start-ups by 1995. New Zealand cannot yet boast such an unprecedented increase. However, with 5.5% of the total women's full-time work-force employing themselves and at least one other, the numbers are increasing and the employment and monetary impact cannot be taken lightly. For example, the

5

business owners surveyed for this book averaged 9.2 employees each, and created an average yearly turnover of almost one million dollars. Understandably, as more women open viable businesses, they will affect the economic health of the nation by creating jobs and stimulating cash flow throughout the nation. Hence, as women attain greater margins of profit in New Zealand, their enterprises should be viewed as necessary components within the economy.

There are many reasons why women are beginning businesses at such an unprecedented rate. The most important evidence lies in the changing nature of the New Zealand and world economy. With a shift in industrial employment from agriculture, mining, and manufacturing to the service sector, an "entrepreneurial" economy has evolved. As New Zealand begins to appreciate the profitable nature of the service industry, small enterprises will — as they are now in the United States — be tagged as the fastest-growing employment sector. Historically, women identify with smaller enterprises, and as the manufacturing sector of New Zealand loses its dominance, the service economy will provide the major outlet for business. Women in the United States and New Zealand are taking advantage of such an economic shift, and using it to establish greater numbers of their own enterprises.

For many women, establishing and owning a business is a relatively new phenomenon. According to 20% of the women surveyed, New Zealanders have portrayed the entrepreneur as a "dirty dealer", "money grubber" or someone who "robbed from the poor." Women were socialised to believe that profiting from one's own business was ill-bred and uncouth. Women were not supposed to work, and they were especially not supposed to like it! However, as society demanded two-income families and as the media portrayed working women in a positive way, more women worked within the company structure. Only when many of those ambitious women began to butt their heads against company barriers did economic independence via entrepreneurship prove a very tasty carrot. Like their American counterparts, New Zealand women are just beginning to realize that ownership is power and that economic parity can only be achieved through entrepreneurship and independence.

6

Entrepreneurial women are now being described as "the new immigrants" in the business world. Highly ambitious — yet displaced — corporate women are speaking a new language. They are opening new territories where a woman can quite adequately blaze a trail. Throughout this book we will discover why these women opted out of the household or company, and what catapulted them into creating their own business. More importantly, I will analyse the typical New Zealand business owner, what barriers she must face and how New Zealand society perceives her. Lastly, the New Zealand business owner will share her experiences with younger women and those women tired of jumping company or household hurdles.

Only when women know the immense possibilities open to them, stake a claim, and mingle with others who "speak the new language" can they aspire to build — and profit from — an enterprise entirely their own. Only then will women be seen acting as catalysts in a more enlightened and dynamic business world.

SETTING THE STAGE

Statistics indicate that the numbers of women proprietors working full-time in the work-force are increasing steadily, concentrated within the service sectors, and becoming established in all major urban areas. Such findings come primarily from New Zealand's governmental statistical surveys. However, one must note that very little statistical research has been carried out regarding women business owners. Utilization of the census figures and statistics compiled by government departments proved the only sources for such information, and unfortunately, very little information could be provided by such agencies. What follows is a discussion of the available statistical material regarding women business owners in New Zealand.

THE RISE OF WOMEN ENTREPRENEURS

As the statistics indicate, the percentage of women proprietors (see Graph 1) working full-time with employees has increased steadily while the percentage of male proprietors with employees has remained relatively the same. Acknowledging the definitional change in the 1986 census of "full-time" work for women from a twenty- to thirty-hour work week, the number of women proprietors from 1981 to 1986 jumped from 4,691 to 25,404, while male proprietors advanced from 62,231 to 83,928. Percentage

GRAPH 1 NUMBER OF WOMEN ENTREPRENEURS IN NEW ZEALAND

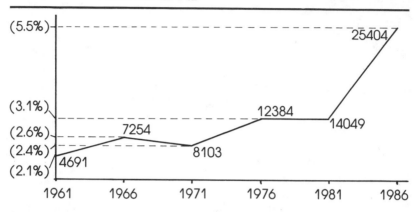

increases for women were 3.4%, compared to the men's increase of only .3%. Both statistics indicate that although males comprise more of the business owner population, women are creating businesses at a much quicker pace than their male counterparts.

GEOGRAPHIC DISTRIBUTION

Understandably, the most popular areas to operate businesses are the major urban centres. As the graphs illustrate, 53.6% of women proprietors operate from the top half of the North Island, and with 26% of all owners situated in Auckland, 'the City of Sails' leads all other New Zealand regions by a margin of 17%. Other urban areas such as the Waikato (9%), Bay of Plenty (7%), Wellington (7%), and Canterbury (8%) also spawn higher numbers of women-owned businesses.

DISTRIBUTION BY INDUSTRIAL SECTOR

As Graph 4 indicates, women work in three major job/career industries. Community, social and personal services lead all areas with the number of women employed reaching 214,200. Wholesale

10

GRAPH 2   GEOGRAPHIC DISTRIBUTION OF WOMEN-OWNED BUSINESSES

Northland	4.8 %
Auckland	25.9 %
Thames Valley	3.3 %
Bay of Plenty	7.4 %
Waikato	9.2 %
Tongariro	1.4 %
East Cape	1.6 %
Hawke's Bay	3.9 %
Taranaki	4.8 %
Wanganui	1.6 %
Manawatu	3.4 %
Horowhenua	1.7 %
Wellington	6.6 %
Wairarapa	1.2 %
Nelson Bays	2.1 %
Marlborough	1.2 %
West Coast	.08%
Canterbury	8.3 %
Aorangi	2.5 %
Clutha-Central Otago	1.95%
Coastal-North Otago	2.8 %
Southland	3.1 %
Total	100 %

GRAPH 3 GEOGRAPHIC DISTRIBUTION OF WOMEN-OWNED BUSINESSES

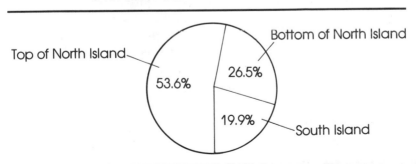

GRAPH 4   DISTRIBUTION OF GENERAL EMPLOYMENT BY INDUSTRIAL SECTOR

Industry Placement	Male	Female
Agriculture, Hunting, Forestry and Fishing	111.9	52.2
Mining and Quarrying	5.3	–
Manufacturing	207.9	96.0
Electricity, Gas and Water	14.7	2.6
Building and Construction	93.5	11.4
Wholesale and Retail Trade, etc.	137.4	158.4
Transport, Storage and Communications	80.8	31.4
Financing, Insurance, Real Estate, etc.	61.8	69.8
Community, Social, Personal Services	162.6	214.2
Not Specified	4.3	3.5
Total	880.1	639.4

and retail trade follows second with 158,400 female employees, and manufacturing third with 96,000. There are proportionately the same number of men in the same three categories; however, unlike women, they are quite evenly distributed in almost all the other divisions listed.

According to these three reviews of statistics, certain trends appear regarding women in the work place. To further document such trends, fifty-seven women owning fifty-two businesses were interviewed. Criteria for the study demanded that the woman 1) had established the business or 2) held majority ownership of the enterprise, and 3) employed three or more individuals. Within the next five chapters, comments and statistical information from the women business owners have been utilized, and later, the profile chapter will describe the woman business owner in terms similar to the findings and statistics outlined above.

It should be made clear at this stage that this is by no means a definitive study, and that statistically valid conclusions cannot be drawn from the number of women business owners surveyed.

2 CATALYSTS

Women are jumping into the work-force at an unprecedented rate. The 1986 census figures indicate that 68% of all women are working and pursuing full-time jobs. Understandably, as more well-qualified women enter the job market, barriers within company and government institutions become more apparent. Almost 40% of the women business owners interviewed believed that specific legislative and corporate barriers catapulted them into business ownership. For instance, while legislation recognised women's viability within the community and encouraged her independence, its weaknesses revealed how much further women had to go to achieve equal opportunities in the work-force. Similarly, as women advanced up the corporate ladder, they encountered subtle discrimination and discovered their initial fast pace had slowed to a crawl. Finally, as 70% of women surveyed indicated, after putting so much time and effort into a company, the ability to make money for others was no longer a challenge. However, although the walls proved too high for some, others used the barriers as steps into the managing director's chair.

GOVERNMENT LEGISLATION

In the past twenty years, the amount of legislation affecting New Zealand women has increased. Although no specific acts regarding businesswomen have arisen, provisions in relevant statutes have aided women interested in beginning and maintaining their own enterprise. Each of the five acts summarized below directly recognises the image of a woman's viability within the workplace; however, the weaknesses inherent within the legislation have also prompted many women to go out on their own.

EQUAL PAY ACT, 1972

Specifically, the Act provides for the "removal and prevention of discrimination, based on the sex of the employees, in the rates of remuneration of males and females in paid employment, and for matters incidental thereto." In essence, the Act guarantees that women receive pay equal to men when performing an equal job under equal conditions.

Although the legislation appears valuable to women in the workforce, it also has several weaknesses. Author Dr. Helen Place contends in her book, *Women in Management: A New Zealand Study*, that the Equal Pay Act does not "necessarily mean equal opportunity because the lack of adequate training . . . confines women's choices to low-level jobs."[2] In addition, any minor change in the title/job/duty circumvents the Act and allows for a legal pay difference. Also, the Act is immensely hard to enforce: implementation by male-dominated unions is unlikely, it is too difficult to obtain redress for unfairness in practice, and the Government provides no officials or statutory body to investigate, assist implementation or enforce the Act. The Act also loses some of its impact due to natural economic and socio-cultural forces: current market wages influence the process of valuing job factors, and most men are responsible for creating the valuation definitions.

The implications of the Act are all-encompassing. In theory, women and men are now regarded as equals in the working world. However, such equality expands far beyond the parameters of work.

With the advent of two-income households, women have begun to call for changes in child rearing and home life. They are demanding increased numbers of child care centres and parental leave involving both individuals. In addition, since women now have some market worth and a "guarantee" of their employability, many have enrolled in university and vocational courses.

Although the Act can be sidestepped, the legislation has encouraged society to re-educate itself and think of women in very different ways. And though women have received guarantees of their worth under the Equal Pay Act, they have also received empty promises. Equal pay does not mean equal opportunities. Without an equal standing in job opportunities, equal pay is meaningless. Hence, as many of the women surveyed for the study acknowledged, their independent careers in business began with the realization that legislation could never guarantee equality within a society inherently riddled with discrimination. Consequently, many saw governmental action as useless, and decided to succeed on their own merits, rather than on the merits of their parliamentarians.

APPRENTICES ACT OF 1972 AND 1983

Two versions of the Apprentices Act tried to guarantee females an equal standing within careers formerly regarded as fitting only for men. In 1972, the Act first allowed girls "to enter apprenticeships in all trades in exactly the same way as boys." By opening up entrance into trades designated as "men's work", women were allowed to enter an environment which allowed them to learn a marketable skill and trade. However, outside the forty trades specified in the Act, women still had to receive "special approval" regarding entry into the trade. Eleven years later, an amended version of the Act rescinded such exclusionary "approval" clauses, and the updated version makes no reference or allowance to either gender. In addition, besides guaranteeing a more streamlined procedure permitting a greater range of apprenticeship opportunities, it also tries to improve the quality of training provided.

Although entrance into the trades had become easier for women, Dr. Place maintained that they still had to confront "entrenched negative attitudes [and] even hostility" within the male-dominated trades.[3] Hence, the legislation gave women a symbol of their equality within the trades, but in fact, the male attitude appeared to dissuade many women from entering such fields.

MATRIMONIAL PROPERTY ACT, 1976

The Matrimonial Property Act re-affirms the legal status of married women, recognises the equal contribution of a husband and wife to the marriage partnership, and calls for a just division of matrimonial property between spouses when a marriage ends in divorce or separation. Overall, the Act stipulates that each partner can claim half of all matrimonial property.

Although the Act provides a basic code promoting fair treatment between both husband and wife, its effectiveness can be minimised by legal wranglings and costly delays over settlements. However, overall, the legislation has proved heartening to married women concerned about equality in the legal system. The Act states that "the rights, privileges, powers, capacities, duties and liabilities of a married woman [shall be] the same in all respects as those of a married man, whether she is acting in a personal, official, representative, or fiduciary capacity." Altogether this section gives her independence and grants her equal standing with those involved in the legal and business world. Such standing allows at least minimal involvement in such areas, and it provides a toe-hold for many women starting again by creating their own ventures on an equal footing.

HUMAN RIGHTS COMMISSION ACT, 1977

The Human Rights Commission Act offers significant benefits to women by prohibiting sex discrimination in the work place. It makes it unlawful "by reason of sex" to "refuse employment" according to gender, to offer different employment or contingency employment packages because of gender, to dismiss an employee because of gender, to treat an individual seeking employment any differently according to gender, and to advertise jobs with gender specifications attached.

Although the legislation looks far-reaching and can be very useful to women in the work-force, it has proved extremely hard to enforce because those who suffer the discrimination are burdened with proving it. Hence, although many of the women know of their rights, only a small proportion appear to use the Act's provisions to defend those rights. Again, although the legislation appears very helpful to women, it merely delineates how much further they have to go to achieve equal standing in the work place.

PARENTAL LEAVE AND EMPLOYMENT ACT, 1987

The Parental Leave and Employment Act prescribes the "minimum entitlements with respect to parental leave for male and female employees [by protecting] the rights of employees during pregnancy and parental leave." Essentially, the Act's aim is to allow both parents to continue their career after having children. The legislation protects the rights of both men and women employees during pregnancy, maternity and paternity leave. Most notably, the Act requires employers to keep the individual's job open — unless a redundancy situation occurs — for leave periods up to four weeks. If the period is extended further, the employer is required to give the individual first preference for openings in similar positions.

In particular, the Act delineates the shared nature of the parent's responsibility to both the children and the household. For instance, the father — in addition to the mother — can receive leave, and the legislation allows one year's extended leave to either parent on a single or shared basis. The legislation emphasises the importance of both child-rearing and job security and states that no dismissal can occur because of pregnancy, use of parental leave, or taking care of an adopted child as your own.

Although the Act appears quite foolproof for mothers wanting to retain their career status, the legislation states that there is no absolute right to resume employment if it disrupts the employer's business, costs the employer extra money, or is of detriment to the other employees.

Overall, having children may have prompted many women to cut the ties with their employer and begin businesses moulded around the needs of their families. Yet for those wanting to stay in their job, the legislation recognized the viability of a woman's career and allowed her some flexibility in returning to work.

UP AGAINST THE CEILING

Just as Henrik Ibsen's protagonist in a *A Doll's House* is surrounded by glass walls and ceilings, so too are many of New Zealand's corporate women. However, many of these high-flying women have opted out, and gone on to create offices where they sit at the top. What is this phenomenon which catapults so many women into their own enterprises? Simply, the glass ceiling is the invisible barrier between senior and middle management. In general, it originates within senior management who promise their top — and often token — women higher positions; however, at the appropriate time, the promotion rarely materializes and is usually put off until "next year." Many of these women see themselves on a company ladder with the position hovering above them, yet a glass barrier separates them from it, and eventually the position is taken by a male regarded as undeserving, who has not yet — according to one business owner — "paid his dues." The following is a discussion with several New Zealanders who found the invisible barrier quite apparent in their companies and opted out to operate businesses of their own.

Little recognition of merit played a key role for many women affected by the glass ceiling syndrome. Nine of the women surveyed stated that if the company had listened, and acted upon some of their suggestions, they would never have gone out on their own. An Auckland architect, now owner of her own architectural firm, said of the company she spent six years proving herself to, "I was never taken seriously at the firm, I rarely received support or even positive feedback regarding my work." In addition, she believed that because she was a woman she received jobs which were unprofitable; hence, when promotions occurred, she was rarely considered a winner because her work was not regarded as highly lucrative or worth architectural awards. "Most of what I received were household jobs. Personally, I would much rather manage and supervise than design, and most of the men I worked with just couldn't understand that. Because they wouldn't listen, and with the onslaught of jobs I wasn't interested in, I had been actually considering re-training for some other profession." She added: "I felt trapped within a Catch-22 scenario: If I complained, I was considered a 'typical' woman, and if I stayed silent I would continue to perform work I was unhappy doing." In addition, she discovered that her firm was encouraging clients to ask that she not be included on jobs. Because she was a woman, both her firm and the clients believed she was not competent in the architectural business. Finally, what really ended her time with the firm was that "I couldn't stand seeing less-experienced men be promoted above me and paid much higher salaries." She stated that if "they had only listened to what I was saying, I would never have left. Personally, I'm not that ambitious. Opening a business was a last resort . . . I didn't want to do it. However, in order to feel I was doing something worthy and verify my sense of self, I had to go out on my own and I've never looked back since." For a woman who has not had to advertise for her architectural services and can boast bringing in two jobs from every one performed, one can understand why she is no longer required to look up to receive kudos from any of her colleagues, and enjoys facing her competitors on an equal standing.

Even prestigious law and accountancy backgrounds cannot guarantee immunity from the invisible barriers inherent in firms throughout New Zealand. As sole practitioners and owners of their businesses, two lawyers and one certified accountant attested that barriers in some firms remain rock solid. According to an Auckland lawyer now acting as a sole practitioner, the partners in her firm "just kept talking about her immediate partnership, but there was never any action." In exasperation, she resigned, and the firm gave her one day's notice, a month's pay and demanded that she clean her desk out that night.

Similarly, another sole practitioner, based in Wellington, left her firm as the most senior woman to establish her own business in Wellington. She resigned from her firm because "after working for six years, acting as the highest ranking woman in a firm with no female partners, and handling higher and higher loads of pressure, there was no indication of partnership." In addition, she discovered the professional climate within the firm was not amenable to women at all. In fact, after disagreeing with a partner on a case which dealt with one of her specialities, she was taken off the case. Afterwards, she heard that one of her colleagues said that with her off the case, he was pleased to "kick a woman down the stairs." Yet the animosity men project towards professional women encompasses a much larger area than just legal firms.

An Auckland-based accountant noted that after qualifying for her accountancy certificate at the age of forty and working with a firm for six years, she ran into the glass ceiling. With an expanding portfolio, excellent rapport with clients, and a high profile, she asked her firm for a partnership. They refused. Staying on for three months more and then leaving to create her own enterprise, she now has 500 clients whom she has acquired in the past two years. She says of her treatment with her past employer: "What really irked me was that after I left, they made partner a young man who had been with the firm for only six months. I couldn't believe such hypocrisy." With the success she has had in attracting new clients every day, neither can her competition.

With a combined tenure of forty-one years, three women left their well-established careers after they collided with the unseen barriers. After six years, one Aucklander exchanged her job as a multi-national advertising sales executive for the position of managing director of a top consumer magazine publishing company. After garnering a record-setting 50% of all Pacific advertising revenue for her past employer, she was told that "according to company rules because she was a woman, she could go no further in the company." She stated: "No matter if I sold 100% of all revenue. I couldn't go any further with this company, and I was sick of hitting my head against a brick wall." Hence, she left the job she had fought so hard for and bought an already established company which she has led through successful expansion while turning over a million dollars. Another Aucklander invested fourteen years in a company before establishing her own business. Undergoing a number of changes of ownership, her company did not feel it could promote her any further in New Zealand, and decided to send her to Australia where she worked within a very male-dominated, limiting climate. After working with a host of patronizing bosses, she decided she was "sick of working for idiots" and asked why she did not "work her guts out for herself." Similarly, a woman who invested twenty-one years in teaching, opted out of a hierarchy which did not allow her the freedom or the recognition she believed she deserved. Hence, she bought a small book and card shop tailored for the young professional. She says: "Although there are always many worries about a business, I left teaching because I had so little input in the decision-making process. Beyond affecting my students, I had very little control or independence within the structure of the job, and there were very few job opportunities for women within administration. Now, I have a job which is extremely rewarding, . . . and I'm always learning something new."

All these women bumped their heads against an invisible barrier instituted in a business world governed essentially by men. What spells their present success was the ability to work within the rules of the system, perceive their own differences, and act upon the market needs. And as a majority of women interviewees noted, achieving success at each level hinged upon her image within a competitive market, rather than the product or service she supplied.

IN THE LOOKING GLASS

Call it reverse discrimination, but statistics indicate that as more women open their own businesses, they employ fewer and fewer men. Of the women surveyed, over half the owners mentioned that their offices either had a "token" male or contained an all-female staff. Margie Thomson in the *New Zealand Herald* noted that as women are opting out of the male, corporate structure, so too are they finding it "more comfortable to leave men right out of their offices."[4] One business owner stated that she would employ "anyone who fitted on a personal level—but that may be more likely to be a woman." When asked why more women "fit in" to an office headed by a female, one business owner said: "In my business, team effort is most important, and men seem too preoccupied with the win/lose mentality. They always have to be right or the best in the office, and if they aren't, then they sulk. My business depends upon a quality product with strict deadlines, and a male's competitive 'one upsmanship' just isn't efficient around here." Another woman contended that she did not hire males because "Women were already discriminated against in employment and she was only helping to redress the balance." However, other than merely "setting the scales right", why have so many women opted out of employing men? How do men react to the woman business owner, and how do men differ in operating a business? More importantly, what distinguishes men from women in the perceptions behind operating a business? What image does the looking glass reflect?

WOMEN ON MEN

One clothing designer and business owner stated: "There are three types of men. The first sees the woman as an individual person; the second is wondering what is under her clothes, and the third is patting her on the head." Such a comment helps illustrate how women perceive and categorize their male colleagues, competitors and employees. According to Margaret Hennig and Anne Jardim's book, *The Managerial Woman*, men react in several different ways once a woman has stepped into "their" arena. The authors contend:

"Depending on a man's own feelings of status security — sexual, social and intellectual, with all of their complex interrelationships — his response may range from welcoming a newcomer with potential brains and ability, to curiosity as to whether she will make the grade, to a need to test whether or not she can, to — in the worst cases of primary sexual insecurity — a determined attempt to put her back where she belongs, to drive her out, to maintain the status of the group as male, as masculine, and thus avert the threat to a precarious sense of masculine sexual identity which the presence of a competent woman evokes."[5]

After studying the responses of nearly sixty women business owners in New Zealand, several categories of men — arising from their response to the woman as business owner — correlated well with the Hennig and Jardim study. What follows is a discussion of three roles men superimposed upon the woman as competitor, colleague or boss.

WOMAN AS PET

According to R. Kanter in *Men and Women in the Corporation*, many men impose the role of pet or "mascot" on women within the company structure. According to the author, such a woman "is expected to stay on the sidelines, and is often subjected to patronizing comments . . . which undermines a woman's self-image and undervalues her competence."[6] However, such a perception does not only exist within the parameters of the company. Many of the women business owners surveyed, complained of the patronizing attitudes they encountered while establishing and maintaining their businesses. Several women with large turnovers and high profits stated that men regarded their business as a "hobby" and something they did for "fun." One woman stated that a friend intimated she was working full-time "just to keep busy" while her husband earned "the serious money of the household." Of the women surveyed, eight business owners stated that patronizing men tried to steer them away from beginning their own business with bits of sometimes well-meaning advice. One financial planner was told that her "place was at home", while another was told it was a "man's world" and a "woman's place did not belong in this trade." One man told a business owner that she could not "expect her business to last", and a woman would never "be able to manage it" because — as another man stated — "if things aren't going well, you'll cry — right?" Others described the attitude of male friends as condescending — especially when these friends asked why they kept "playing games" as they "set up shop." In sum, one owner stated that many men in the working world "just don't take women business owners seriously."

WOMAN AS OUTCAST

In tandem with being seen as plush toy pets, successful women business owners said some men perceived them as "freaks" and "outsiders." 20% of the women interviewed believed men see them as "money-grubbers" because in New Zealand society, according to one woman, it "is not socially correct for women to make profits." However, according to one owner managing her public relations firm, the only way to live with being considered an "oddity" was to be "the best in the field." Over 50% of the women interviewed said they had to be "twice as good as their competitors" because a woman's "failure is remembered much longer than a male's."

24

80% of the women interviewed said they had to continually prove themselves in fields dominated by men. Five of the women directly stated that they felt pressured to relieve the fears of men who appeared "unsettled" and who "were terrified to deal with a woman", by proving their merit and undergoing "cross-examining sessions" in order "to win confidence and respect." Upon the first contact, eleven of the women surveyed stated that most of their male clients viewed them with "suspicion", and one woman stated that she believed she was given a difficult time because "Some men just didn't want to see me succeed and come through." However, such an attitude sometimes drove women to try even harder and prove their credibility. One woman stated that men "underestimated her, called her a 'stupid' woman" and she "became so angry" that their "scoffs egged her on" to create a business which within five years became their major competitor within the market. Like an increasing number of women, she was asked to step into the "inner circle" and be considered by her male colleagues as an equal partner within their world.

WOMEN AS EQUALS

"When my male colleagues first met me, they used adjectives like 'pushy', 'agressive', and 'slick'. They thought it was obscene for a woman to trade in stock worth five million dollars. However after six years in the business, I now appear to have earned their respect, and I'm treated like everyone else." After several years of "proving up", over half of the women business owners believed males viewed them as equals and viable competitors within their market. One owner of a textile manufacturing business stated that "males in her field respect a woman with a brain, and they look at each person differently." Laughing, she added, "Now I always get what I want." Another woman dealing in hotel supplies noted that some men prefer dealing with women. She said: "Decent guys have always given me a go!" Another woman with a business in legal research stated, "I knew my business was going to work, and what really helped me was the attitude of the lawyers I worked with. In Wellington, I hold a unique position in a service which is beginning to explode. Being a woman has never worked as a disadvantage against me, and working with solicitors has really been great." A business owner marketing her training and public speaking skills, noted that her gender has been an asset because "I'm the only full-time woman on the speaking circuit, and that makes me unique and marketable." However, the best example of men supporting a woman colleague with marketable skills comes from a story told by a market researcher in Auckland who, after resigning her position with her employer, opened her door one day to find personal business cards and letterhead lying on her doormat. One of her clients believed in her market potential, to the extent of designing her business logo, and asking that his business be her company's first client.

As the next division indicates, men and women may operate differently and see different values in their business. The management of profit, power, and risk determines the way a business is operated and how "successful" its owner is. What follows reveals several ways women — in comparison to men — view their enterprises, and the way such views dictate the growth of themselves and their businesses.

WOMEN v. MEN: PERCEIVING A DIFFERENCE

Over 50% of the women surveyed indicated that the business would not be a lifetime venture. Several said they did not want the business to become "too big an animal" and take over their lives. Others said there were so many other challenges in life to conquer — owning a business was just "one chapter" of an expanding book. Why do women opt out just before a business may promise to balloon and reap huge rewards? According to American authors Sarah Hardesty and Nehama Jacobs in *Success and Betrayal*, women have been given so many choices in their lives that if they choose a career it will have "exacted a price — a trade-off — in the caretaker role at home."[7] Hence, women — unlike men — yearn for a job which will compensate them at both the intellectual and financial level. Unlike men who are given few choices but to work and "shoot for the top", women demand more from a career because of what they must give up to pursue it. A woman believes that if a position is no longer "fulfilling" her, she has the right to opt out, and try another challenge. Hardesty and Jacobs call such a phenomenon the "learning curve mystique", contending that the "significance of a job and women's happiness in it is measured not just in titular and salary terms . . ."; a woman "measures success in how much she grows from or is enriched by the experience."[8] As one business owner stated: "I can see myself leaving this business in six years because I don't want it to expand too much. When I've made enough 'dough' and will be able to maintain my standard of living, I want to get out of it — there are so many other things to do." A top real estate agent/business owner said: "It's the controlling of growth and knowing what to do in the middle years that is tough. I'm caught between staying small, selling everything or expanding two or three times my size. If I opt for expansion, I may receive great monetary rewards for it, but my family may suffer, and I don't know if I want to be tied to this business for the next twenty years." Finally, one woman has taken her learning/ growing needs seriously, and at the time she leaves her extremely successful public relations business, she hopes to enrol at Oxford University!

Staying small in the market indicates women's and men's conflicting views regarding profit and independence. Ten of the women interviewed said they retained "a hands-on" approach to their business, and preferred to stay small because they could oversee, manage and participate fully in the venture. Proudly, one woman said: "Ninety percent of the time, I control the business. Unfortunately, the other ten percent controls me." Such a statement exemplifies the way women prioritize independence above financial rewards. According to Hardesty and Jacobs, "Women's definition of success, unlike men's, has little to do with money. The game is still independence, with money merely the means to the end. Money represents control over their environment; men take that control as a given. For men, economic security is merely the price of entry in a game where the real prize is power."[9] Although

27

one study suggested that women and men were equally interested in obtaining power,[10] two American authors state that both genders define power in different ways. As their study indicates, where men rank profit as their key motivating force, women rate independence as their first priority. Hence, women, unlike their male counterparts, are not as concerned with "building empires . . . [because] they work more for income than for wealth."[11] Not surprisingly, the ways women perceive their income, especially as they start up a business, dictate the ways they view the risk.

Over 34% of the owners surveyed believed that at many times in their business career, they were reluctant to take risks. Many saw risk as a factor which could kill the business and therefore destroy their income and lifestyle. According to Hennig and Jardim, "Women see risk as entirely negative. It is loss, danger, injury, ruin, hurt. One avoids it as best one can. And there is yet another dimension: men see risk as affecting the future; it is risking one's potential, risking future gain, risking career advancement. Women see risk as affecting the here and now, what they have so far managed to achieve, all that they have."[12] Unlike men, women are socialised to "play it safe" and such an attitude is most apparent when women speak of financing their business. One business owner noted that she "never tried to ever borrow money for the start-up of her business." She stated that she wanted to be "cautious" because she did not like "borrowing other people's money." Another said: "I undercapitalized my business so much because I didn't want to go into debt. Of course, I made my life much harder because without capital, how could I expect to succeed?" Another woman who quit her business said her lack of risk regarding finance partially killed her business. She stated: "I operated on a cash flow, which is not that efficient because I only had enough money to do the next order but nothing if I wanted to make something I thought might be a future big seller. Financially, I was always in the black, and I always paid my bills on time, but I believe the conservative way I viewed money did not help my business."

As has been shown above, men and women view their businesses in very different ways. If women see their businesses primarily as jobs offering independence and challenge, men see them as

28

profit-making vehicles. Yet each complements the other. Between the brother and sister there exists a healthy tension; however, the problem arises when the other sister enters the arena.

WOMEN v. WOMEN

If women business owners intimidate a major portion of their male colleagues, how do other women react to a "sister" sitting in the managing director's chair? According to the women business owners surveyed, 21% believed other women — especially their friends — reacted to their position with jealousy. One business owner named such a phenomenon the "Cinderella Complex", which is a modern-day scenario depicting all the ugly sisters fighting among themselves as they try to undermine their potentially successful sister. Agreeing with the theory, one business owner said "Women are harder on women. And [in comparison to men] women are even more threatening to each other." Why is it that women appear to sometimes be their own worst enemy? An approriate answer lies in the business owner's apparent disregard for her nurturing role, and the non-business woman's seeming dedication to it.

Six business owners complained that several women continually remind them of their families, question their dedication to the business and instil them with guilt as they juggle both a family and a career. Overall, non-business owners questioned the way the business owner prioritized her business, husband and children. One woman noted: "Quite a few women have made me feel guilty operating a business while my husband takes care of the family. In fact, once as I was doing a presentation, and asked for questions regarding the product, one woman stood up and asked me point-blank who was taking care of my children. I answered, 'You can have them!' I didn't hear anything more from that woman again." Another business owner said women with children make her business ownership a real issue because they believed she was sacrificing her family for her career. Lastly, one owner jaded by her frequent business contacts with other women, noted she places all the women she meets into two categories: "achievers or people who just sit around dwelling on real or imagined injustices." She added: some women may not be able to have both a family and a business, but "you get what you deserve" and if you can handle both, then why must women who have chosen one path begrudge others who have chosen two or three?

One theory directed towards successful corporate women, may apply to the women business owners' experience, and help explain the competitive and disapproving tension female owners experience when confronted by a non-business owner. Roger Gould in *Transformations: Growth and Change in Adult Life* contends that successful women — unlike their counterparts who are raising full-time families — enter and compete within "a rough and tumble corporate world [which] taps women's competitive drive for power, revenge, and status — a sometimes voracious appetite so long denied to them as good little girls . . ."[13] Because they are no longer acting as "good girls", they are perceived as "oddities" imprisoned within a society demanding they take a nurturing role while also demanding that they work.

Yet why do even successful professional women castigate those who have entered their own business? One non-business owner working within a firm employing men and women stated that she believed women entering business on their own was a "cop out." She stated: "Those women were so promising in their fields, and once they have opted out of the firm they must give up advancing their specialties, and perform 'general practice' legal services. In addition, by opting out of their firms, the younger lawyers have lost excellent mentors." One woman agreed with her colleague's statement and added: "By opening my business, my 'top' potential has been lost. But you choose what you lose — right? On the bad days, I may accuse myself of 'copping' out, but I enjoy my work, the flexible hours, and the ability to direct my own life. But most importantly, I know I made the right decision, and anyway, I'd had it working with men."

The Queen Bee Syndrome also helps explain why some women view their independent "sisters" with a wary eye. The queen bee theory builds upon the "woman as nurturer" role model for women, and maintains that within society women hold the position of power within the family. However, as her supreme position or vocation is, as Hennig and Jardim would say, "challenged" by the independent careerist, she becomes insecure because her dominant position is threatened.[14] Hence, non-business owners see their successful counterparts as a threat to their societal role in New Zealand. And the tension mounts as increasing numbers of younger women opt into their own ventures, confident they can be everything to everyone. But can they? What suffers most with the woman business owner, and how do they see themselves within their business? Is business ownership really the cherry on top of the sundae?

WOMAN v. BUSINESS: MY BUSINESS, MY SELF

Fulfilment, flexibility, freedom, an "evangelical desire", and a host of other answers provided reasons why many of New Zealand's women began their own enterprises. Yet what is hiding beneath the "silver" lining? How do these women see themselves within the business world? If many of the women will not play the nurturing role in society as wife, how do they play the role of mother to their bouncing business? How does their "baby" feed off them, what kind of care does it require, and what do they receive in return?

SUCCESS AT WHAT COST?

At least 75% of the business owners surveyed, believed their ventures demanded sacrifices in their lives. Whether it was personal time or outings with their family or friends, something was lost. In terms of time, effort, and compromise, one business owner noted that "most women just have no concept of what it takes to operate a business." Another owner, proud of her flourishing venture, said: "Someone came up to me once and said, 'You're really lucky to be so successful.' I answered, 'No, I'm really lucky to have a body that's able to work damn hard.' " One third of the business owners believed the "discerning public" underestimated pure, hard work. Said one business owner: "There's no such thing as easy money." Another owner said she had to "work like hell" to maintain her business, while another said that with all the work she had to do both with family and business, she "would love to have a wife." However, working seventy hours a week may not always be the answer. One business owner with a turnover of ten million said: "Working hard doesn't necessarily mean working smart. No matter how hard I work, many times I learned my lessons the difficult way: they all cost me money." With a smile she added: "Usually, I don't make the same mistake twice"

According to over 50% of the women surveyed, personal time is overrun by the businesses' needs. For many, that meant loss of marriage, friends, family, and bouts of stress and loneliness. Commented one business owner: "I have an excellent standard of living, five profitable businesses, and a caring family." Then she paused and added: "But you know, I have no friends left. I just have no time for them, and they have just drifted away." Another owner stated: "Some of my friends call me up expecting me to drop everything and go out to lunch with them. They think it's 'naughty' when I refuse, but what can I do — I'm directing a company which just turned over $3.5 million this year." As a result of the owner's dedication to her business, one unmarried woman conceded: "I've got all the trappings of a successful businesswoman, but I believe owning your own business is extremely lonely." And if the loneliness does not bother you, the stress may give you more than a few sleepless nights. According to one owner: "I was undergoing huge stress loads, and I did not know how to get rid of it. I realized I just had to stand back, re-assess the businesses' needs against mine, take some relaxation courses, and I was on my way again."

PERSONAL ATTRIBUTES

Although hard work aids in the survival of businesses, all the interviewees believed many more attributes and much "care" were required to maintain a successful business. One owner noted:

"Although I believe the phrase 'Girls can do anything', I also believe that working in New Zealand's business world requires lots of courage." Another woman added: "I never thought there were ever any barriers to opening a business." However, in hindsight, she said: "I've learned that New Zealand women don't like the aggressive, 'boss' role. They would much rather take second stage to someone else. However, what New Zealand women must learn, is to overcome the 'boss' stigma and gain confidence in their own leadership and ability to wield power effectively." Several owners stated that Kiwi women must be more "positive", "value their market worth", "never accept limitations", and learn "to make their needs clear, and say 'I want.' " Another owner added: "New Zealand women have to learn how to ask questions." Financially, other owners noted that "the ability to risk", "having a good financial base" and "choosing and maintaining a good financial advisor" is very important because he or she "can really determine your success." Lastly — on a more positive note — one owner said: "Take your business seriously, but not yourself."

Although the life of the woman business owner may not amount to celebrity billing, for many women the benefits appear to outweigh the disadvantages. As was illustrated above, the commitment and sacrifices may prove detrimental; however, 40% of the women surveyed commented that after having a business, they "could never work for someone else again." One woman summed up the mixed feelings of her "sisters" by commenting wryly: "In one year, I believe I have three suicide days, three miserable weeks, three hectic months, and the rest is wonderful!"

Besides hard work, 80% of the women business owners agreed that before their business grew to be "wonderful" their success or failure was determined by their venture's financial backing and economic credibility. And such financial support only materialized once they entered the revolving doors of a bank.

4 GETTING THE FINANCE

Before becoming what most of them considered "successful", over 80% of the women surveyed had to enter a banking institution and ask for a loan. After presenting their projected cash flow charts, banking histories and other relevant financial data, over half did not receive direct loans *per se*. Rather, overdraft facilities, and co-signatures from either spouse or family, provided funds for the majority of novice women business owners interviewed in New Zealand. As one woman said: "I had my husband co-sign because I wanted the money for the business. It hurt my pride, but my major objective was receiving financial backing and beginning the business." However, according to the owners themselves, financial institutions became assets as women became financially credible business owners and began to expand their ventures. One Auckland-based manufacturer said: "I wouldn't be where I was today without my bank manager. She has really concentrated on my financial needs, and has gone out of her way to help me. For example, when I was thinking of expanding, she travelled to one of my potential sites. I rely on her, and I now feel comfortable to expose myself and the company to her advice. We work as a team."

Yet what about those who do not advance to "first base" with the bank? Why did 20% of the women interviewed believe at least one bank did not "play fair" as they considered her loan application? How is the bank manager viewed by the potential owner who is refused or must make concessions to receive a loan, and more importantly, how does the bank manager view the woman who just walked through his door?

SEEING THE BANK MANAGER

Five of the women surveyed complained of patronizing bank managers who obstructed them as they asked for the financial support needed to begin or expand their businesses. One woman owner who left her business said: "I had the chance to export my product overseas, and it was guaranteed a fantastic marketing blitz in England. However, when I approached my bank manager with the plans and all the information regarding the product's promotion, he looked up and said: 'I've seen women like you with plans for little boutiques, interior decorating, and antique shops, and frankly, you're all bad news.' I was devastated. Only later did I receive a co-signed overdraft from my husband's banker, but by that time the promotional bit went on without me, and all my overseas opportunities had disappeared." One owner said she felt the bank manager treated her like a "half-witted shit" and she came out of the session "feeling that small." Several women business owners underwent clashes with bank managers. One owner said her bank manager — after seeing the appropriate cash flow charts and evidence of ability to finance the loan through assets — treated them as though their effort was just an exercise in "fun." She said: "He became an obstruction in a business which was beginning to turn over a quarter of a million." After presenting a bank manager with the appropriate financial data, another partnership of women were asked if they were "really serious about this." Would a man be asked such a question? Lastly, one owner said she refused negative replies to her loan applications. She said: "I had to make them believe I was serious. I was expanding, and I kept asking them how they could expect a million dollar turnover with a $10,000 overdraft. I didn't let up. In fact, I received their confidence and loan, but I think I almost battered them to death with all my calls."

While it may not work well in other cases, making banks know you are serious and being single-minded in your approach can be a true asset. Although no bank managers want to be hounded, they like displays of commitment. One banking executive said: "Bank managers are risk managers. Unfortunately, women do not always appear to be the best risks." Another bank manager responsible for a loan portfolio in the millions, said: "Whether male or female, when a bank is risking thousands of dollars, I want applicants who have done their homework. For instance, some of the best women clients I have give me their curriculum vitae, a list of their businesses' current projects, her current client base, the operating philosophy, business objectives, plans for the upcoming year and mortgage payment information. All this information is supported by projected budgets, cash flows, balance sheets, and revenue statements." She added with a smile, "My women clients are extremely conscientious, and outstrip the male clientele in presentation."

Besides acting as risk assessors, bank managers depend also on their intuition when approached by a loan applicant. One manager said: "I need quite a bit of 'paper' from my potential clients, but what I essentially depend upon is my gut feeling regarding this person. Do I trust this individual? What determines whether they receive the loan is their ability to present themselves and their information." Another bank executive said: "Banks are trying to help people. We don't try to put up brick walls." However, said another executive, "Many of the managers in their fifties are a product of their environment, and many may unknowingly discriminate against women. Yet whether the person wears trousers or a skirt, if they have no assets, the bank is less prepared to take a risk on them." And unfortunately, as another bank manager agreed, many women opening businesses — in comparison to men — have very few assets.

Although all the bank executives agreed that their women clients were extremely "reliable" and "conscientious", they also agreed that many potential female business owners may not have the experience or management skills to operate a business at full capacity. One executive noted that many women he saw may not have researched their market, and did not have a viable business plan. Another said many women undercapitalize because they are "cautious and less prepared to take a risk." He added: "In many cases, if a woman appears committed but a bit misdirected and confused, I send them to an accountant." Finally, one executive noted that some women misjudged the types of people they employed during growth periods. She added: "Jumping from a business which is turning over five million to twenty million in two years is a big step, and many women continue to manage their businesses with objectives and plans they have outgrown. They must 'think big' and surround themselves with people who can think in the same context."

One business owner said whenever she approached the bank, she gave off an "aura of knowing what she wanted" and after "speaking the banker's language" she usually emerged from the bank with a loan. As more women begin to follow such an example, and become better educated — at either the academic or experiential level — in business and financial management, more financial institutions will be forced to commit themselves to helping women open, maintain and grow with their ventures.

5 PROFILES

Who is the "typical" woman business owner in New Zealand? After three months of interviewing fifty-seven women maintaining fifty-two businesses in both the North and South Island, several trends have appeared. What follows is a discussion of owners' responses to questions regarding family ranking, education, marital status, number of employees, category of business, parental influence, demographic area, and the date business began. In all cases, the women were divided into two categories: those with a one-million-dollar or more turnover (13), and those with less than a one-million-dollar turnover (39). An average of both is also displayed. To qualify as members of the study, business owners had to 1) have begun the business or 2) hold majority ownership of the business, and 3) employ three or more individuals.

SINGLE SEX/CO-EDUCATIONAL SCHOOL

As graph 5 indicates, an average of 67% of the women interviewed attended a single sex school. Without male competitors in the classroom, 20% of the women interviewed believed their schooling

38

GRAPH 5   SCHOOL TYPE

$ Value of Turnover	Single Sex	Co-ed
One Million & above	79%	21%
Below One Million	67%	33%
Total Women	70%	30%

allowed them more "freedom, and independence." One woman noted that her school "pressured its students to succeed" and another stated that the "independent" teachers provided her with "role models." However, 17% of the category believed the single sex school was limiting because — according to one woman — "it never taught me to think." Another businesswoman noted that she believed her school had "plenty of limitations, and it never enabled me to be creative." When asked if their school provided them with any particular business skills or if the schools ever talked of business as a vocation, 75% of the women answered negatively. Said one woman: "Our schools did not talk about business. The successful careers either were in the medical or law fields, or a bit lower to a nurse or teacher level."

Although only a small number of women attended co-educational schools, very many defended their choice by echoing one woman's statement: "If one must compete and work within a male-structured society, why start your schooling in a single sex and artificial setting? Working with males in a co-educational environment provides valuable lessons for many young women entering the work-force and society in general." Unlike her mother, one woman said: "I'm putting my kids in a co-educational school. It may mean that they won't be seeing most of their friends from the neighborhood, but by having to meet kids from other 'walks of life' I believe it will allow them to grow. In addition, the school provides them with such a flexible amount of classes and careers. They have so many choices that I never had!"

FAMILY RANKING

It is no surprise that the first-born or eldest child of the sex is more likely to begin a business. American authors Margaret Hennig and Barbara Hackman studied women enrolled in the M.B.A. program at Harvard Business School in 1963-1964, and discovered that twenty out of twenty-five women were first-born children.[15] In addition, the study revealed that a first-born child — according to the behavioural dynamics — was accorded a "special" status within the family. Their study also revealed that the eldest child had a closer affinity to her father. They note: "The father-daughter relationship provided an added dimension to these women's childhoods. From it they drew attention, approval, reward and confirmation. It was an added source of early learning, a very early means of expanding their experience, and through it they gained a role model with which they could begin to identify."[16] Although current studies now give less credence to such a father-daughter link, one New Zealand business owner stated that the Hennig study clarified her relationship with her father. She stated: "Dad never had a son, so . . . as the eldest, I became my father's 'surrogate son' in the family."

What proved most interesting are the equal percentages of 36% accorded to both the youngest and the eldest when turning over a million dollars or more. Throughout the world, no other study has shown such a trend. One business owner tried to explain it by saying: "As the youngest child, there were no barriers and I believed I could do anything." Perhaps as the "baby" of the family or the last of the sex, the younger children both receive more

GRAPH 6   FAMILY RANKING

$ Value of Turnover	Eldest	Youngest	Middle	Only
One Million & Above	36%	36%	14%	14%
Below One Million	53%	33%	12%	2%
Total Women	49%	33%	12%	2%

attention from and are less restricted by the parents. In fact, the business owners ranked youngest in the family appeared in their interview more flamboyant, communicative, and able to take risks at both a higher level and a younger age than did the middle, only or eldest children.

MARITAL STATUS

It is not unusual that 57% of the women turning over one million dollars or more are either single or divorced. According to a survey done by the *Wall Street Journal*, executive women "are less likely to be married than lower-ranking peers. 32% are single." The article added: "These women are the most likely of all those surveyed to feel that they have had to give up something to achieve success."[17] In many cases, says Hardesty and Jacobs in *Success and Betrayal*, successful women opt out of marriage, and instead become "married" to the company. They continue that as " 'corporate bride', the woman . . . has elevated corporate affiliation to the level of surrogate lover — a loyal, steady, reliable, and endlessly challenging companion in a fifty-fifty partnership."[18] One divorced New Zealand business owner said: "I was married once, and now I'm not. I don't really believe I need a husband now. He would be another demand in my life, and my business takes up enough

GRAPH 7   MARITAL STATUS

$ Value of Turnover	Single	Married		Divorced	
		Children	None	Children	None
One Million & Above	36%	21%	21%	14%	7%
		43%		21%	
Below One Million	21%	54%	9%	7%	9%
		63%		16%	
Total Women	26%	45%	12%	9%	9%
		56%		18%	

of my time right now." Another business owner stated, "I'm single, I have a thriving business, and I have five godchildren! Even if I don't have a husband, I'm surrounded by people who care about me, and my business has provided me with friends and clients of all ages." Lastly, one woman said: "Having a business is relatively lonely, but my employees are excellent: they are my family. One Friday night I had a big warehouse fire, and do you know, all my employees came out on Saturday morning — without being asked — to help me clean it all up? These people take care of me."

With 56%, married women maintain a slim majority over their single "sisters." However, when one compares American statistics indicating that 90% of all male corporate executives maintain a marriage, one wonders if such a New Zealand statistic is much of an accomplishment. Can a woman be an effective wife, mother and business owner? As shown on graph 7, half of the married women turning over one million dollars or more opted out of having children. Yet how did the mothers cope? "I have a nanny and a part-time gardener," said one business owner with four kids. She added: "And I work like hell." Over two-thirds of the married women with young children stated that they used some sort of day-care facilities. Over 75% said they employed nannies either full- or part-time. One woman organized her business so she could concentrate on her children for part of the day, and only took on clients willing to do business during her scheduled times. She said: "My kids are extremely important, and I want a healthy balance in my life. I have had to turn down business, but work shouldn't be everything in your life."

EMPLOYEES

"I see myself in this business as creating employment," said one business owner. According to the statistics, it appears her colleagues feel the same way. With women business owners turning over a million or more, fourteen people — on the average — receive jobs. All other business owners can boast an average number of

GRAPH 8   BUSINESS CATEGORY

$ Value of Turnover	Service	Product	Manufacturing
One Million & Above	38%	54%	8%
Below One Million	62%	36%	2%
	98%		
Total Women	56%	40%	4%
	96%		

eight employees. Such statistics help verify the importance of women's businesses within the economy and the labour force.

SERVICE, PRODUCT, MANUFACTURING

As was described earlier in the book, New Zealand is participating in a trend towards a service economy. Out of fifty-two businesses, only two provided a manufacturing base.

PARENTAL INFLUENCE

For 63% of the women surveyed, having a parent working within the business world acted as an asset for many of the women owners. The Hardesty and Jacobs study asserts that where "fathers head a family business", daughters — currently successful corporate women — become more aware of the business's "tangible substance, responsibilities, products".[19] Over half of the women in each category believed that a family member's — father or otherwise — presence in the business world contributed to their success. One business owner commented that "Dad had a business, and he always took me with him to see the lawyers and the accountants." Other women grew up with mothers running businesses, and several owners commented that a grandparent provided them with a viable role model. Said one owner: "My grandmother owned three shops, and I grew up seeing her manage these businesses.

She was firm, honest, and she had a top-quality product. She was an excellent role-model for me."

EDUCATIONAL BACKGROUND

As graph 9 indicates, a majority of successful women business owners went to — according to one owner — "the school of hard knocks." With 64%, a large majority of women turning over a million or more attributed their success to working themselves up through a company. However, as one women said, "After seeing fools at the meetings, I thought 'maybe I'm better than them.' " Echoing such a statement, one woman began her business by saying: "If I make it for others, then I can make it for myself."

Although only one woman held a degree in commerce, with 21%, those with a background in teaching were very well represented. According to one business owner, a "successful career" managing a business hinged upon the skills found in teaching. She noted: "Teaching is an excellent grounding for business because it provides leadership, motivational, and organisational skills." American authors Hardesty and Jacobs try to explain the trend in a different way by saying: "Choosing teaching, for the pioneer generation of corporate women, was in many ways a non-choice, a means of postponing the ultimate redefinition of their lives from a traditional to a career role. Many women eventually outgrew that career crutch and went on to successful careers."[20]

GRAPH 9   PRIOR EXPERIENCE AND BACKGROUND OF OWNERS

$ Value of Turnover	Degree	Polytech	Teaching	Work Experience
One Million & Above	14%	7%	14%	64%
Below One Million	23%	26%	23%	28%
Total Women	21%	21%	21%	37%

GEOGRAPHIC DISTRIBUTION

In terms of the volume of business transactions, easy access to national and overseas markets, and population, it is understandable that Auckland holds the largest number of women-owned businesses. With an average of 64%, the "City of Sails" is a clear winner. With such a large market to satisfy, the variety of businesses spans enterprises in qualitative market research, personnel and travel agencies, textile manufacturing, data express services, engineering, architecture, public relations, real estate, importers and distribution agencies, furniture installations and contracting, printing and publishing services, accountancy, legal and financial services, airline brokering and plant tissue nurseries for overseas exporting. And the list goes on. With more markets and a greater number of higher disposable incomes, Auckland is the city where — if handled properly — service-intensive businesses can multiply and make viable profits.

Wellington is the home of the public service; and with legal services and research agencies, public relations and training, archive management, hotel suppliers, environmental and planning services, and specialist retail shops, 23% of the business owners found their niche servicing this city where government plays a key role.

Christchurch remains a very conservative place for women to establish businesses. Overall, the businesses are in areas generally considered a female's domain. Most business owners ran enterprises in catering, bridal and fabric boutiques, fashion, floral boutiques, small retail shops, home entertaining, and furniture manufacturing.

GRAPH 10 GEOGRAPHIC DISTRIBUTION OF BUSINESS BY CITY CENTRE

$ Value of Turnover	Auckland	Wellington	Christchurch
One Million & Above	77%	23%	—
Below One Million	59%	23%	18%
Total Women	64%	23%	13%

In a city filled with tourists, but with few outlets to overseas markets and a relatively small population, it is understandable that women are opting for businesses which are relatively "safe" and guaranteed to make nice incomes, but not necessarily large profits.

DATE OF START-UP

As graph 11 shows, 67% of the women surveyed entered their business in the last five years. With an economy increasingly dependent on service industries, and more women rushing into the work-force, it is not surprising that the numbers have ballooned so quickly. In terms of de-regulation, one business owner said: "When the Government de-regulated the airline industry, it was an excellent time for me to begin and expand my travel wholesale business. I could now work with individuals who, because of competition, became more professional and were expected to negotiate prices rather than have established fees. It is a much more dynamic environment." Another woman noted: "When the state-owned enterprises were created, it meant more corporations which required consultants, trainers, and better public relations services. With such a move, the Government freed up the system here in Wellington, and we are receiving quite a bit more business." Finally, one woman remarked: "As the economy gets worse, the better my business becomes. As corporations begin to pare down their staff, they bring me in. What would you rather do: pay five people to sit there doing nominal work, or pay me for whatever time I use on your account?"

GRAPH 11   DECADE BUSINESS WAS ESTABLISHED

$ Value of Turnover	1950	1960	1970	1980	1983-88
One Million & Above	—	46%	23%	30%	54%
Below One Million	3%	8%	18%	10%	62%
Total Women	2%	6%	25%	13%	54%

Although an uncertain economy and a Government full of change may bode well for these business owners, what do they see as their economic future in New Zealand, and what do they believe would make it easier for them — and their younger "sisters" — to trade in New Zealand? Answers to such questions could dictate how many women enter the business world and diversify their nation's economy.

6 REFLECTIONS IN THE CRYSTAL BALL

With mounting numbers of women entering a work-force driven by service industries, this nation must prepare itself for an increasing number of women spawning their own businesses. What can be done to help more women survive the rigours of ownership, and become viable players in the economic arena? Several financial planners commented: "Some women don't seem prepared, both financially and personally, to operate a business, and we try to give them as much financial 'muscle' as possible." And as more women begin to publicly 'flex' their marketable muscles, the economic environment will be forced to notice that it is full of women determined to use their power. Can society's view of the woman business owner change? One American businessman noted that although change is imminent, "This is an evolution, not a revolution. . . . And that doesn't happen overnight."[21] Yet how can more women encourage their sisters to "breed" a business, and hasten the transformation?

According to 20% of the business owners surveyed, women require better access to networks. Several of the women agreed that access to professional women's organisations such as Zonta, Women in Management and the Business and Professional Women's Association provides a forum and "stomping ground" for professional women. However, they believed such organisations failed to touch women who had not yet "made it" into the business or professional arena. Hence, six owners suggested that women in business could increase their numbers and networking ability by establishing an agency tailored for potential and established women business owners. Information regarding start-up and business maintenance would be provided, and it would also prove an excellent arena for all owners to meet and work with each other. Said one owner: "We need an organisation providing women with an 'old girl's' support network. Such a network would enable others to mingle with women acting as role models for others and instilling a positive, 'can do' attitude in each other." As another owner said: "Women in business require good sounding-boards, and who knows the heartaches of a business, but another business owner?"

40% of the owners believed their financial burden could be eased by governmental or financial initiatives. According to economist Suzanne Snively statistics regarding women in business could increase dramatically if greater forms of financial support were provided. Says Snively: "It is understandable that as many experienced women opt out of the work-force and become chief executives of their home, they also consider the position of business owner as an alternative to re-entering the work-force. What stops them is the lack of finance and capital backing." What is the solution? Ideas regarding women's banks and venture capital associations geared for women have surfaced in New Zealand only to be buried again. Yet as viable women's businesses gain both visibility within the economic arena and credibility within women's business organisations, they will be provided with a voice in the financial arena.

Several of the business owners interviewed believed their sisters could succeed much more readily in the business world, if they forgot some of the rules "mother" taught them. Said one owner: "Women are always taught to be liked. In most families, confrontational and assertive behavior are not encouraged. However, in this business you can't be over-sensitive and you must develop a very thick skin." One woman, picturing herself in the role of helpmate and nurturer, said, "I never believed I would actually open my own business until I prepared the business plan. I'd convinced myself that I was doing it for someone else, never myself." Another owner said: "Women were never taught to take control of their lives. A man was always supposed to be dominant, make the decisions and 'take care' of the woman." Hence, because women saw themselves as appendages of men, one owner stated: "Most women are just too scared to try opening a business. They don't think it is possible." On the other hand, another woman said she combats her fears by thinking "problems just don't exist. I tell myself they are all merely challenges with alternative solutions." Lastly, said one business owner, women have grown up with an inferiority complex and think their skills are less valuable than a male's. Said she: "Once you open a business remember to value your abilities. Believe what you do is equal to what a male does, and deserve to be compensated as a man's equal." Agreeing with such a comment, an owner said: "When I first started out I felt I couldn't charge as much as men. When I realized how much a male colleague was charging out to clients, I said 'I couldn't charge that!'." Smiling, she added: "I soon outgrew that idea."

As more women "outgrow" their inherited societal values, and accept the responsibilities of running a business, they will — in time — become a credible constituency within New Zealand. Numbers should increase as more enlightened women appear out of glass ceilings, jump over governmental hurdles or emerge from the household. In addition, as powerful coalitions form, and women begin to express their concerns regarding business and financial initiatives, society will be forced to view them as credible participants in the economic arena. If, as one business owner stated, women are prepared to make sacrifices for their own venture, it can reward them with large degrees of independence, flexibility, creativity, and satisfaction. Although increasing numbers of women note the risk involved, they also see achievement and monetary rewards as a fitting compensation. As more women surround themselves with the enigmatic aura of business ownership, so too will they realize that economic parity can only be achieved and guaranteed through entrepreneurship and independence.

NOTES

1   Sarah Hardesty and Nehama Jacobs, *Success and Betrayal* (New York: Franklin Watts, 1986), p. 279

2   Helen Place, *Women in Management* (Auckland: Motivation-Inc., 1981), p. 97

3   Ibid., p. 99

4   Margie Thomson, "The Rise of the Entrepreneusc", *New Zealand Herald*, February 16, 1988.

5   Margaret Hennig and Anne Jardim, *The Managerial Woman* (Garden City, New York: Anchor Press/Doubleday, 1977), p. 171

6   Marilyn Davidson & Cary Cooper, *Stress and the Woman Manager* (Oxford: Martin Robertson & Company Ltd., 1983), p.25. Taken from R. Kanter, *Men and Women of the Corporation*, (New York: Basic Books, 1977).

7   Hardesty and Jacobs, *Betrayal*, p. 237

8   Ibid., p. 35

9   Ibid., p. 210

10 Harish C. Tewari, *Understanding Personality and Motives of Women Managers* (Ann Arbor, Michigan: University Microfilms International), p. 26.

11 Hardesty and Jacobs, *Betrayal*, p. 288. Quoted from Bettner and Donahue, "Now They're Not Laughing", p. 118.

12 Hennig and Jardim, *Managerial*, p. 27.

13 Hardesty and Jacobs, *Betrayal*, p. 112. Quoted from Roger L. Gould, *Transformations: Growth and Change in Adult Life* (New York: Simon & Schuster, 1978), p. 259.

[14]   Hennig and Jardim, *Managerial*, p. 149.

[15]   Ibid., p. 76. Quoted from Margaret Hennig and Barbara Hackman Franklin, "Men and Women at Harvard Business School" (unpublished MA research paper).

[16]   Ibid., p. 80.

[17]   Hardesty and Jacobs, *Betrayal*, p. 269. Quoted from "Achievement and Ambition Typify Younger Executives," *Wall Street Journal*, October 25, 1984.

[18]   Ibid., p. 39

[19]   Ibid., p. 60

[20]   Ibid., p. 74

[21]   Ibid., p. 139

BIBLIOGRAPHY

Davidson, Marilyn & Cary Cooper: *Stress and the Woman Manager*. Oxford: Martin Robertson & Company Ltd., 1983.

Hardesty, Sarah & Nehama Jacobs: *Success and Betrayal: The Crisis of Women in Corporate America*. New York: Franklin Watts, 1986.

Hennig, Margaret & Anne Jardim: *The Managerial Woman*. Garden City, New York: Anchor Press/Doubleday, 1977.

Place, Helen: *Women in Management: A New Zealand Study*. Auckland, New Zealand: Motivation-Inc., 1981.

Tewari, Harish C.: *Understanding Personality and Motives of Women Managers*. Ann Arbor, Michigan: University Microfilms International, 1980.

APPENDIX 1
PUTTING THE PIECES TOGETHER: HOW TO BEGIN AND MAINTAIN A PROFITABLE BUSINESS

Although women may now be opting into business ownership at a speedier rate than their male counterparts, they must realize that — regardless of gender — only one out of five new businesses survives the first five years. Although such statistics may not appear heartening, they do encourage any aspiring business owner to do her homework before entering the world of business ownership. With the help of the Westpac Business Advisory Service, this section has been written for aspirants wishing to minimise their risk by first examining themselves and their need for business ownership. In addition, we will see how successful businesses hinge upon the owner's knowledge of her product, the market, the competition, and upon her own financial acumen. Only after examining such motivations and factors can owners hope to "beat the odds" and work on the winning edge of business ownership.

EXAMINING THE SELF

It is extremely important that an enterprising business owner define why she wants to maintain a business. For instance, does she want to maintain independence and flexibility within the work-force? Or does she merely want to provide a community service which others will pay for? How profit-oriented is the owner, and is business growth important? How essential are job and family security?

To be successful, a potential business owner must develop her abilities in the marketing, operational, financial and management areas of the business. Yet as the owner copes with all these facets, she must also have the staying-power to work in a business which may not show profits within the first few years. Called the "stickability" factor, the business owner's degree of commitment remains the vital ingredient for a business's success. To determine whether or not you "have what it takes", let us examine this factor and the entrepreneur's necessary responses.

The degree of commitment and the stickability factor are sometimes most affected by factors outside the business. For instance, if the owner is married, how committed is her husband to the business? Would he be willing to take over some of her household tasks, and would he be prepared for her to work late more often? Do both spouses know how business ownership could affect their relationship? Is she, like half of the women interviewed for this study, willing to risk a marital break-up?

Women with children must also examine a business's role within the family. Is she willing to live, like a large percentage of the women interviewed, with guilty feelings as she rushes off to care for her enterprise? Can and does she want to be effective in both roles? In addition, are she and her family prepared for their living standard to possibly drop, and is she prepared to mortgage all the family possessions for the sake of a business? Is the family willing to forgo a holiday for quite some time?

Lastly, a woman must examine her own strengths within a business. Is she unafraid of confrontation, and willing to ask innumerable questions? Can she lead and persuade people to do things she wants done — and take notice of reasons why there are better ways of doing them? Can she work long hours, forcing herself to continue? Can she deal with boring repetitive jobs, and handle knockback after knockback from clients without giving up? Most importantly, can she insist on what she wants, rather than give into someone else? Can she stand her ground?

If a woman has answered negatively to any of these questions, she must think twice about business ownership. The business world is not for the faint-hearted, and bankruptcies and liquidations, besides being costly to the pocketbook, can also destroy business credibility and self-confidence. Additional research — besides the information supplied by the interviewees for this book — delineates five personal characteristics common to all financially successful business owners. For instance, the profiled business owners never began projects they did not intend to finish, and they preferred moderately difficult situations to very risky ones. In addition, they regarded monetary rewards more in the manner of a "scoreboard" against which to measure their performance than as an end in themselves. Success also hinged upon the owner's choice of business associates. Research showed that successful associates were chosen to complement the business owner's strengths. Allies were not chosen because they were family or friends. Lastly, successful business owners appeared very aware of their economic environment and the subtle shifts in the market.

KNOWING THE MARKET

The first step in establishing a successful business lies in knowing the market you are entering. Before introducing any idea, service or product onto the market, a business owner must determine if her product/service is needed or wanted, and if she can adequately satisfy such a need or want. To answer such questions, an owner must query the individuals involved in her potential market. She must ask her friends, family, and the neighbour down the street if they would use the product. She must go to the possible outlets where her service or product would be sold, and quiz the shop owner on her idea. She must also examine her potential competition, and determine who has the competitive advantage. In addition, the potential business owner must ask herself what are the pitfalls or advantages of marketing this product or service? By asking questions about the market, the aspirant can determine the feasibility of the idea and the parameters of her success within the market. However, she must remember not to give the idea away: very few rules exist in the business world.

In order to further determine the feasibility of the product or service, the potential owner should write down answers to specific questions such as: Who are my customers, where do they get their income, and what proportion of their income do they spend on products like mine? In addition, she must estimate the number of national and regional customers in the market area, and estimate how frequently they would purchase the product or service. Then, the aspirant is required to study her competition in the market area and ask: What is the nature of the competition in the market area, to what extent does the competition satisfy local demand, and can I increase the demand for the type of product? Most importantly, the aspirant must ask herself what realistic share of the market her product can snare within the first, second and fifth year.

Small business experts say that the success of a business lies both in its product's image and in location. No matter how innovative or time-saving the service, if it lies hidden in an alley-way and encourages little media or word-of-mouth advertising, the business will die a quick death. The potential owner must determine how much she wants to pay for advertising and she must look at what her competitors are doing. How can her product appear different from that of her competitors? What is the most effective advertising tool?

Many of the women interviewed said that media advertising made little impact in their market. Rather, a large percentage commented that word of mouth through good service realised much of their additional business. True, as noted earlier in the book, women may have to work harder to gain credibility within the market, but they may also have to pay much less for their advertising and pass such savings onto their customers. At the start-up stage, a business owner may have to weigh up high advertising costs and higher visibility versus a lower, more competitive price and a market visibility dependent only upon good service and word of mouth. Re-analysing the owner's expectations for the business and her definition of success may provide the answer for such a marketing dilemma.

One of the more pivotal questions regarding the product or service is its life cycle. Any business owner must ask herself how long her product or service will last in the market. Typically, a

GRAPH 12   THE BUSINESS LIFE CYCLE

A Typical Product Service Life Cycle

Sales volume curve and profit margin curve in relation to a product's life cycle.

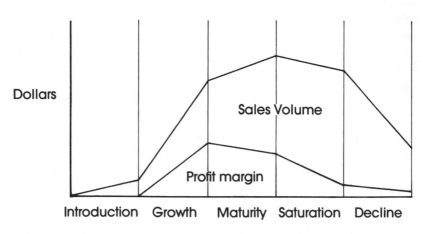

Typical Phase in the Life Cycle Curve

Introduction Market development, characterised by low sales volumes and slow growth as the product is adapted to the market's requirements. The cash flow over this period is nearly always negative and many products never get beyond this stage.

Growth A rapid growth phase, where demand outstrips supply. The growth and margins during this phase usually attract the attention of additional competitors and both price competition and market segmentation are likely to occur.

Maturity Decreasing growth rate, occurs when sales begin to decline and manufacturing or servicing capacity catches up to demand. Profit margins begin to level and shrink.

Saturation Sales stagnate, characterised by levelling of the total dollar value of sales. Unit sales increase, but price erosion occurs. The declining margins and intense competition force some suppliers out of the market.

Decline   The downward trend, the product/service begins to become outmoded or superseded by more attractive alternatives. Only a few suppliers remain and the product has completed its life cycle.

product/service life cycle goes through five stages. As the graph illustrates, the introductory stage is characterised by low sales volume and slow growth. Profit and cash flow are usually negative, and unfortunately many products never pass beyond this stage. In the growth stage, demand outstrips supply, and growth margins at this stage usually attract the attention of additional competitors and produce intense price competition. This stage moves the business from adolescence to adulthood, and again, unfortunately the business which enters the race last may have to drop out first. As one interviewee said: "I wouldn't be here today, competing with the 'big boys' if I didn't have quite a bit of capital support from my family. The price cutting was intense, and I lost quite a bit of money at this stage. The trick just lies in hanging in there, pumping money into the business, and hoping your customers believe they are receiving much better service for the price they are paying." At the maturity, saturation, and decline stages, the growth rate decreases, capacity catches up with demand, sales begin to stagnate and the product or service eventually becomes outmoded and is replaced by a more attractive alternative.

Charting a product's life cycle allows business owners to plan for the future. Re-directing profits into other markets with different products or services, can keep a business running smoothly; however, a financial or business plan must exist to keep the business financially in line with the owner's wishes. Knowing the financial side of the business is essential in operating a business, and if the potential business owner is not willing to spend time poring over balance sheets and calculating figures, she must have an accountant or financial planner with a good track record to do it for her. Financial experts can make or break a business, and buying into talent is essential for a successful business operation.

However, for those wanting to do it on their own, the next section describes a business/financial plan, and the way it helps direct a venture's growth in the market.

THE FINANCIAL/BUSINESS PLAN

A good business plan is invaluable to the business owner. Besides acting as a chart delineating the direction and growth of a company, a well-orchestrated plan is the key to encouraging financial backing from investors. What follows is a discussion taken from the MIT Enterprise Forum discussing the business plan's all-important structure.

According to Forum members, the first impression a business plan conveys can be pivotal to receiving funding from financiers and bankers. Investors are looking for evidence that the owner treats her own property with care — and will likewise treat the investment carefully. In other words, appearance can be as important as the content; hence, good form reflects good content and vice versa.

Although each plan — like its corresponding business — should be unique, there is a basic structure one follows when creating a financial plan. With an added executive summary, and table of contents, the core of the plan should not be too long or wordy; however, it must encompass the major aspects of the business. Understandably, it must be presented to potentially the most receptive financiers to avoid wasting either party's time. The bulk of the plan should discuss, in chapter form, nine major sections: The company's background and history, the market, the product, sales, development and engineering of the product, manufacturing, financial data, the investment, and the appendix. The information needed to write such sections will be discussed below.

1) THE COMPANY
This chapter should answer questions regarding the company's origins, expectations, and the owner or management team. It should summarise the enterprise's overall objectives so that the investor

60

receives a clear indication of where the company is going and how it plans to get there.

2) THE MARKET
Define your market in this section, and describe the benefits to the user of your company's product or service. Investors want evidence that founders have a clear idea of who will purchase the company's product or service and why. Spend quite a bit of time on this section: Forum members maintain that exhaustive knowledge of the market gains favourable attention from potential investors.

3) THE PRODUCT OR SERVICE
The third section describes the company's services or products. The operation of the service or product, and any information regarding the patentable functions of the service or product should also be noted. The Forum stipulates that this chapter should be shorter than the market section, further stipulating that the owner should realise the priority of markets over products.

4) SALES
After reading descriptions of the business's market and its product or service, investors want to know how the company plans to approach its client base. This section should outline the ways the product or service will be sold — whether by sales representatives, distributors, in-house salespersons, direct mail, or executive selling. However this section is presented, it must be logical and concise.

5) DEVELOPMENT AND/OR ENGINEERING
Again, the Forum comments on the size of this section, advising that the chapter be brief because the development of the product or service should be well advanced. They note that investors want their money to go into manufacturing and selling rather than into developing a product that is not yet ready to be sold. However, any information offered regarding engineering in support of

manufacturing is well viewed because such an expense should be translated into better products and increased profits.

6) MANUFACTURING

This section should encompass the business's make/buy or supply/demand decisions. All supporting information outlined throughout the plan can be used. Investors want to see the maximisation of profit, and therefore, use of the most efficient and inexpensive manufacturing processes will be viewed favourably.

7) FINANCIAL DATA

This section should summarise all financial projections, and any previous financial performances. It should describe cash flow relative to selling expenses (i.e., wages, material costs), variable expenses (i.e., advertising or marketing expenditures), fixed expenses (i.e., insurance, rents, interest), and personal expenses relative to the owner's financial involvement in the business. This section is extremely important, and it is advisable that an accountant or financial advisor help in its creation.

8) THE INVESTMENT

The last formal section should cover the entrepreneur's expectations of the investment itself. It should indicate how much money the company is seeking to raise, the form of investment being sought, and how the funds will be used.

9) THE APPENDIX

Included in this section should be the owner's curriculum vitae and any background information regarding any of her key employees or members of her management team. In addition, if companies have already been approached and have agreed to become one of the business owner's clients, it is advisable to include their name, and a short synopsis of the enterprise.

After creating a detailed business plan, encompassing all aspects of the proposed company, success is far from guaranteed. Profits may not come before the first or second year of start-up, and most of those monies merely get fed back into the hungry child's mouth. If, as most financial companies suggest, a worthwhile return to the owner does not appear before the end of the fifth year, they suggest abandoning the business. As one of the interviewees said for this book: "You should be in there for a profit. If you aren't receiving a viable return for all your effort, have the courage to close it."

Many enterprising women have had the courage to give up their "baby", but not without such a loss providing them with some of their best learning experiences. One owner noted the business failure she suffered gave her the incentive and the necessary information to begin plans for another venture. Understandably, most women do not want to undergo business failures in order to incur more knowledge regarding business ownership. Hence, the easiest route to knowledge appears in the vital form of the network.

APPENDIX II
BUILDING A NETWORK

In an age where managing change is the top priority, networks providing marketing advice and information are a hot commodity. This study offers considerable advice, and its participants have widened the range of career choices for other women. The term "equal opportunity" becomes much more meaningful as more women become aware of the array of choices and opportunities open to them. Yet for women thinking of business ownership, it must be taken a step further, where ownership becomes an everyday reality. Enterprising young women need to speak with business owners — not merely read about them. Acting as "touch and see" forums, networks are also extremely useful to owners themselves. Business rarely occurs just in the office, and organisations allowing women to mingle and "do business" are vital to creating a more effective and encompassing executive network.

Hence, as an aid to those women wanting to network with their equals, and for others who would like to join their ranks, a list of businesses owned by women is appended. I wish to acknowledge and thank the women whose companies appear below. All these leading business owners either participated in the study as an interviewee, or because they could not fit the study's specific requirements, became consultants for the book. Each of these women gave me their time and energy, and candidly divulged experiences knowing such information would become public. I hope they are as satisfied with the outcome as I am.

AUCKLAND

Alkemi
Allen Realty
Barbara Kirkbride
City Typesetters, Ltd.
Claire Chambers and Associates
Contract Assembly, Ltd.
Corporate Resources Group
Data Express
Designstore
Diane McAsey, Ltd.
En Ambiance
Gain Personnel Ltd.
Gilli Fashions
Grocer's Review
Hamling & Marlow
House of Toys
International Beverages of New Zealand, Ltd.
International Press Ltd.
Kay Hawk Research Ltd.
Kenyon Woodstoves
Lewis and Callanan
Lyndale Nurseries
Margaret Franklin and Associates
Margaret Maylor and Associates
Mobile Art Hire
Multiflora
New Zealand Business Speakers Bureau
North Shore Nursing Services
North Shore Personnel
Qui Direct Marketing
Rick's Café Americaine
Scientific Supplies
Susan Naylor, Ltd.
Textile Network

Tiena Pratt and Company
Trend Travel
Tricia's Total Coordination
Wendy Pye, Ltd.
Worldwide Air Travel
Yvonne J. Watson and Associates
Auckland Regional Chamber of Commerce
Gardner, Bradley, O'Neill, financial planners
Westpac Banking Corporation

WELLINGTON

The Academy of Elegance, Ltd.
Andrea Thomas
Clarity
Consultus NZ, Ltd.
Environmental & Planning Associates
Gilmac Agencies, Ltd.
Kit Clothing Company
Logos Consultants
Jill Moss
Julie Thorpe Accessories
Robin's Agency Services, Ltd.
Rosemary Collier
Second Winds Sportstuff
Simone Garments
Tina Symmans and Associates
Vibrant Handknits

CHRISTCHURCH

Cartouche
Culinary Arts Centre
Home Entertaining
Love in a Basket

The Preservatory Fruit Company, Ltd.
Russel's Fabrics
Sitrite Chairs
Strawberry Fare

PRINTED BY WRIGHT AND CARMAN LTD, UPPER HUTT, NEW ZEALAND